Survival M
Alpha

----

21 Tactics, Hacks and Techniques to Survive Anywhere and in the Worst

Bradley Luther

BRADLEY LUTHER

THE ULTIMATE SURVIVAL WAR

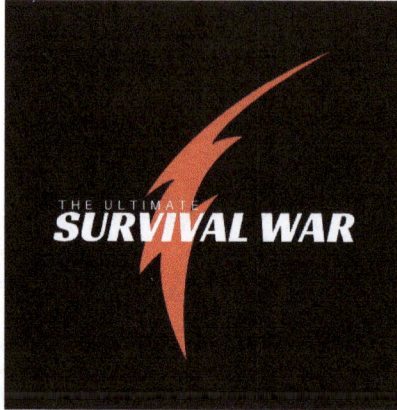

Bradley's story begins at the young age of 10 when he becomes passionate about nature, particularly the forests present in North America.

He immediately has an unconditional esteem for the fantastic documentaries of the legendary Bear Grylls and decides to undertake the same type of career.

Thus, equipped with backpacks, flashlights, video camera, and courage, he begins to explore some of the most fantastic forests until the disaster happened ...

Over 72 hours stuck in a cave, with no food and little water left.

For him and his team, it could really be the end but fortunately they were rescued by local rescuers who were passing through...

This terrible experience provides the motivation for Bradley to start all over again with a series of complete survival guides of any kind.

So, if you've decided to venture into the forest this weekend, you might want to read at least one of his guides to make sure everything goes smoothly!

Table of Contents

Introduction:

This is the kind of survival book that will tell you how to survive anywhere in the world. Survival manuals have always been a big help for people who think they can do anything no matter what happens. With these tips, you can definitely survive anywhere in the world. Survival manuals have always been known to be good aids in times of emergencies and other unexpected things in life or doing adventures. In this book however, you will be provided with the best ways to survive in any kind of emergency situation.

When it comes to the techniques to survive anyplace in the world, there are several things that you have to know about. One of these is about food and water. You must have water available all the time. You must never run out of provisions. Another technique to survive anywhere in the world is about clothing. You must always dress comfortable as possible.

When it comes to survival guide, the techniques to survive anywhere in the world also include the shelter you need to live. You must learn about emergency shelters that will give you ample protection from the harsh weather conditions and from bugs and other insects. If you do not learn about these shelters when you are a survivalist, you will surely be sorry.

These are the best techniques to survive anyplace in the world but what if there was no survival guide? What would happen then? You will surely starve to death right? Definitely. So what do you

need? The techniques to survive anyplace in the world are provided to you in this survival guide.

You do not need to have any special skills for you to survive. All you need is your confidence and boldness to face any hardships that come along the way. A lot of people lacked the confidence and the courage to face their hardships. They are just like timid mice running around in the dark. But you can change that now. Get your survival guide now and start taking life one step at a time.

This survival guide provides you with the best techniques to survive anyplace in the world. Survival does not need to mean dying. It simply means surviving whatever comes your way. This guide will provide you with the courage, confidence, and the skill you need to survive. Learn more about it today. Read more about it online or buy the book.

Chapter 1: Importance and 10 Survival Tips

1.1 Why it is important to learn how to survive in Wilderness

Wilderness survival can be one of the most challenging adventures of anyone's lifetime. Being in the wild and with nature can be an extreme experience.

There is a wide range of arguments answering the question 'Why is Wilderness important?', available on different websites! Arguments come from a very pragmatic sources but also using many emotional arguments, for example :

1.Wilderness Provides Biological Diversity For Both Animal & Human Survival:

Many dangerous animals, plants and microorganisms only find important living and retreat areas in Wilderness. Cross-linked biotopes also increase survival chances for migratory classification.

2. Wilderness for climate protection is critically important:

Healthy forests, moors and flood-plains have a moderate effect on the extreme weather patterns of climate change. It permanently reduces carbon dioxide (CO_2) from air. They give creatures space and time to maintain new climatic conditions to ensure the survival rate of living organisms.

Let's discuss top 21 survival skills and other things you might want to know if ever you find yourself stranded in the great outdoors. These are some common-sense factoids and pieces of life advice that we feel you should consider before you go off on an adventure

Number 1: How to attract attention with a signal or a signal fire

Learning how to attract attention with a signal or a signal fire can be very useful in many different ways. One way is to use it as a signal to draw someone's attention to your vehicle. This can help get your car or truck

parked faster, and it can also help you get into a parking space more quickly. Moreover, if you have your signal fixed to warn you of a fire in the area, you can use it to draw attention to a hotspot. The flames from a fire can be quite bright, especially if they are burning close to your vehicle.

Many people who are rushing to get away from a fire may want to use their signal fire to signal to others that they are far away, but they may forget to do so while running towards the fire. In this case, using your signal fire can help others see your location so you can move closer to safety. It may also be necessary for you to run towards the fire if it has spread so that you can get closer to your car before it catches on fire.

Attracting attention with a signal fire is also useful when trying to stop a person from getting out of an area. If you want to stop someone from getting out of a busy area, you can do this by pointing your signal fire at them. Some vehicles may also have "spitter" detectors that can also distract an individual who may be trying to get out of the car. These devices can be used in a similar way to fire extinguishers in that they can distract and warn someone of danger in a place where safety should be the first priority.

As a general rule, knowing how to attract attention with a signal fire should be done before you are ever involved in a fire. If you are in the middle of running towards your car when a fire suddenly breaks out, you can be distracted by the sight of flames and may not see what is really happening. This means that you may not be able to get out of the way in time and may end up hitting the fire. If you are approaching or leaving a building, when you are entering a building, you will want to look around and make sure there are no hazards in the area that could cause you to trip or fall. You should also make sure there are no people lurking in the shadows of the building. Remember that even if you are using a signal fire, some buildings may not allow you to light the structure with a fire extinguisher. In this case, you may need to use another method to scare away intruders or other dangerous individuals. As long as you follow all of the laws surrounding the area, you should be able to safely get into and leave a building.

If you are stuck in a wild area or a forest, then the dead trees in the wild area can be used as a signal fire as they will burn very well. Want to get rescued fast of course, you do first things first.

Gather any combustibles you can find like tinder, kindling and firewood and set up on a hilltop or in a clearing to get maximum visibility. If you don't happen to have matches or a lighter on you, create a spark using a mirror or a magnifying glass and the Sun.

In a pinch your car battery could work too. If you have none of those handy you can always go the old-fashioned route and bang two rocks together or rub two sticks together.

When you hear a helicopter or plane start piling on the branches, the dryer, the better. This will make the smoke thicker and more visible. Do your best to keep the fire going until rescue comes.

You need to make sure that you always use your signal whenever you are in a potentially dangerous situation.

Make sure that you always have the time and place to practice these methods. If you do not practice your flaring techniques, you will never know when an opportunity will present itself so you will have to react prematurely which may end up creating a dangerous situation for everyone involved.

Number 2: How to keep up your dental hygiene

You're stuck in the wild but that doesn't automatically make you an animal. You would want to keep those pearly whites as pearly white as possible and avoid infections or diseases.

So, here's a simple rundown on how to brush your teeth using only things found in the forest as your toiletries.

Find the twig of a non-poisonous and fibrous tree and use that to scrape the gross stuff off your teeth. Obviously, you won't be able to find toothpaste in the wild so you can boil the bark of any tree with tannic acid which includes oaks, birch, hickory, aspen or poplar and use it as a substitute for mouthwash.

It doesn't taste good but you shouldn't care about that. You can find some SAP and chew on that to get all the gunk out of your mouth. If all else fails, just find a stick and chew on it which will clean your teeth as you chew. Just roll it around and chomp on it to get those fibers loosened up.

Number 3: How to tie a bowline

If it's your first adventure, chances are you've never tied a knot other than your shoelaces. It's okay we can work with that all you really need to know to survive in the wild is how to tie a bowline which is an old but easy to tie method of securing rope that can lift a huge amount of weight.

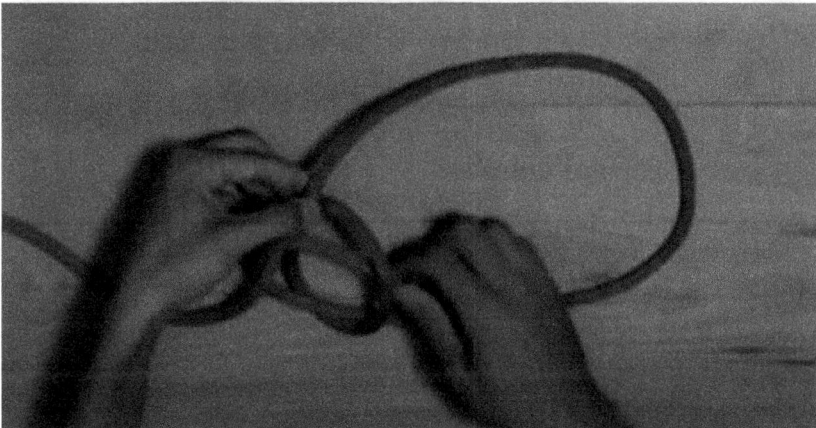

Real outdoor type people use a mnemonic device about a rabbit coming out of his hole running around a tree and jumping back into his hole to remember how to tie a bowline knot and the rabbit comes up out of his hole goes around the tree and gets scared and goes back down his hole and there you go.

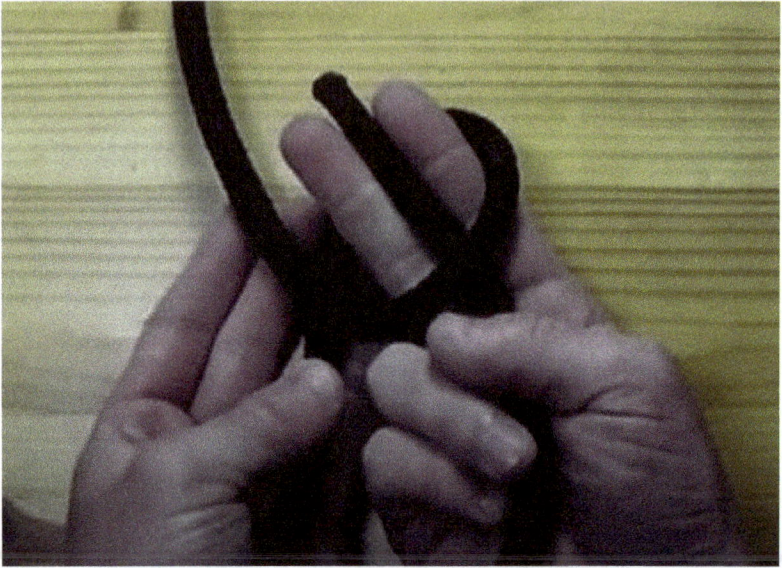

What does that mean? In essence you've got to make a loop near one end of the rope pass the other end of the rope up through that loop. Move that end behind and around the upper part of the firstend and then pass it back down through the loop.

Number 4: How to find your way by day or by night without a compass

In the old days, people would use a needle and a map to find their way in the wilderness. They knew (or had learned) how to use these tools to find their way in a foreign land, but now we do not have to use these tools just to find our way in an unfamiliar place. We can find our way just by reading a map or a compass (some still do that), if we know where to look. But for some of us, knowing how to find a way without a compass or a map may seem like more fun. After all, wouldn't it be easier to find your way when you don't need those tools anymore?

Of course, we do not have to rely on a compass anymore just to find our way in the wilderness. We can use Google Earth, the free satellite map program, to help us find our way. There are interactive maps available online, that let you explore the world without relying on your compass.

You need to get off the grid, though. If you live in a modern city, you won't find yourself in the wilderness any time soon. Even if you do get off the grid, though, you will still need a GPS unit to get where you're going. You need to make sure that you have a way to navigate back to civilization.

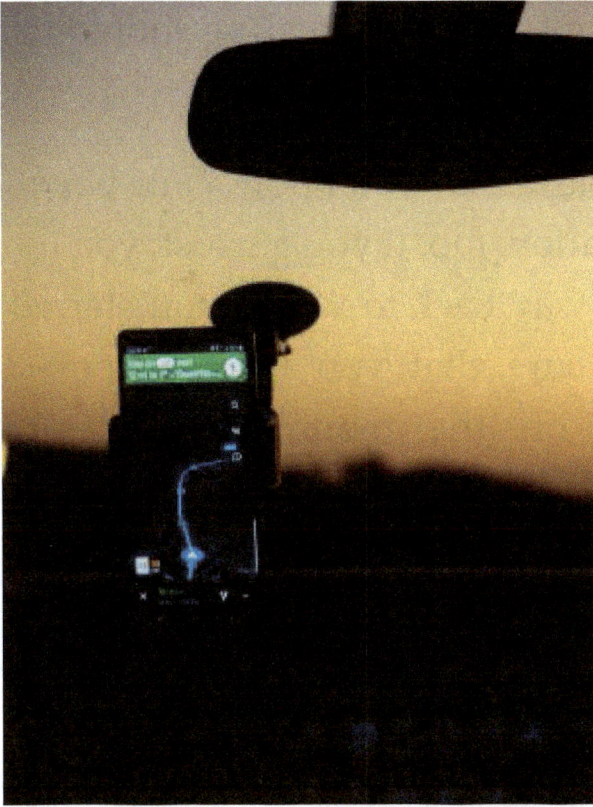

Fortunately, there are some things that you can do to find your way without a compass or a map. First of all, make sure that you can see your way clearly at night. This is especially important if you are traveling through some dense forest. If you are traveling through the woods at night, you need to be able to see your path very well in order to avoid getting lost. Your map, your flashlight, and your hearing should help you a good deal.

Make sure that you know your way back to civilization, too. If you get lost, you'll have to find a way back to where you started from. Make sure that you have a contact high above on the mountain that you'll be climbing to make sure that you have a way back to the base camp.

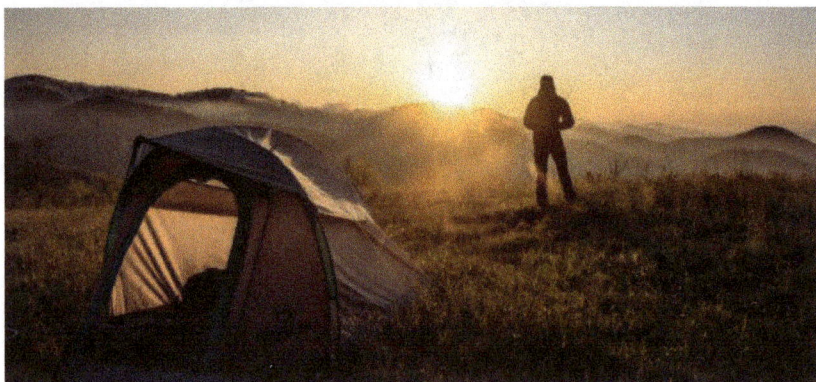

Of course, the most important piece of information on how to find your way by day or by night without a map is this: 'Have a good route planned out before you go'. This means that you have to decide where you want to go, when you want to get there, and how you'll get there. If you plan properly, you can go in an organized and smooth fashion.

Now, let's suppose that you have no preparations, so we have to use those old traditional methods in that case. If it's daytime and you have an analogue watch handy you can use that as a compass. Hold it horizontally, if you're in the northern hemisphere, point the hour hand at the sun. If you're in the southern hemisphere point twelve o'clock at the sun.

Bisect the angle or draw a line midway between the hour hand and 12:00 o'clock and you'll find the north/south line, depending on where you're located.

If you don't have a watch look straight up into the vicinity of the sun. It rises from the east and sets towards the west wherever you are. So, you can use that as a good starting point.

What about night time?

Just find the Little Dipper, now find the Big Dipper. Then imagine a line between the two stars at the furthest part of the Big Dipper and connect that line with the handle of the Little Dipper.

This is where you'll find the brightest star which is Polaris or the North Star and it represents the true north.

Number 5: How to perform DIY first aid

When you think of DIY, the images that come to mind are usually construction workers using long tweezers to mend light fixtures or drills in the hope that they'll nail a new door into the wall.

While any amount of effort can be applied to the DIY process, those who want to learn how to do it properly should practice the basics first. Improperly applied DIY first aid skills can result in serious injury if they're not fixed right away. There are numerous ways to ensure that any attempt at DIY first aid is as safe as possible.

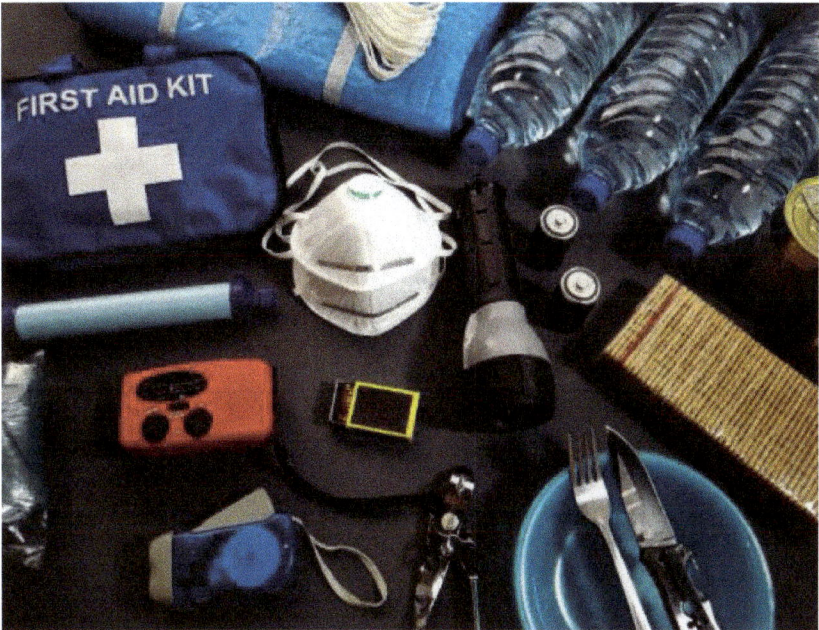

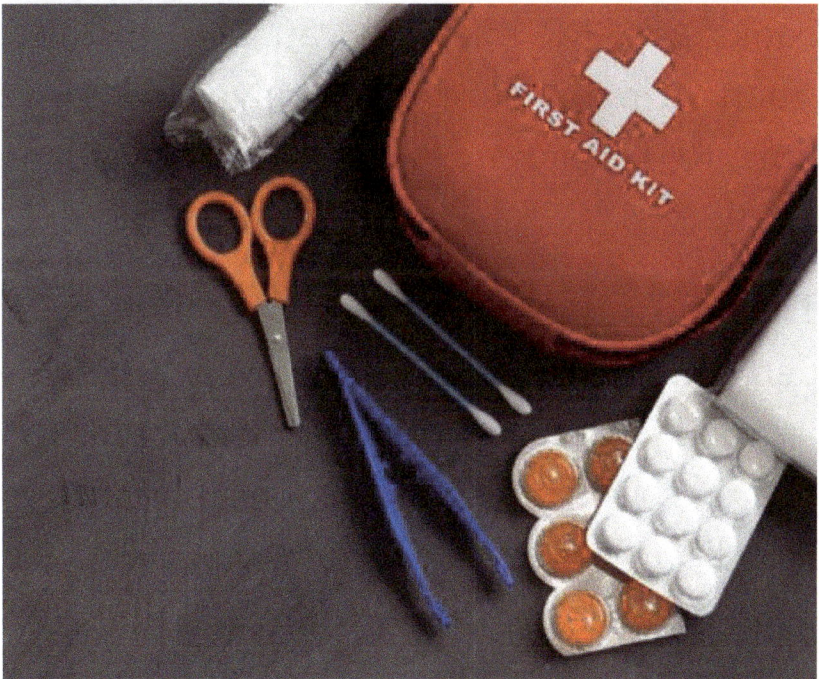

It's important to be aware that the skills involved with DIY first aid aren't the same as those learned from medical courses or from the skills and crafts section of a local home improvement store. If you were to try and learn how to use CPR, for instance, you'd need to train for a year before you could even attempt it on your own. That's because CPR is an extremely specialized skill that only trained professionals should ever attempt to apply. Similarly, while there are plenty of books on CPR that you can buy, it's also smart to make sure that you've had some time to learn how to use the techniques safely.

The best way to get started learning how to perform DIY first aid is to either read about it or talk to someone who's done it before. If you're reading up on it, ask questions at your local library or bookstore, and look online for instructional videos. If you can't find any instructions in print, look online for videos showing you the basics.

Cardiopulmonary Resuscitation (CPR) as a first Aid:

Once you've learned the basics, it's time to move on to the more advanced methods. One important thing to remember when you learn how to perform CPR is that you should never leave an injured person to die. Even if you think you've done a good job at keeping them conscious, if they stop breathing you have no business keeping them that way. As far as how to do CPR yourself, start by holding the person's hand and moving it towards their chest.

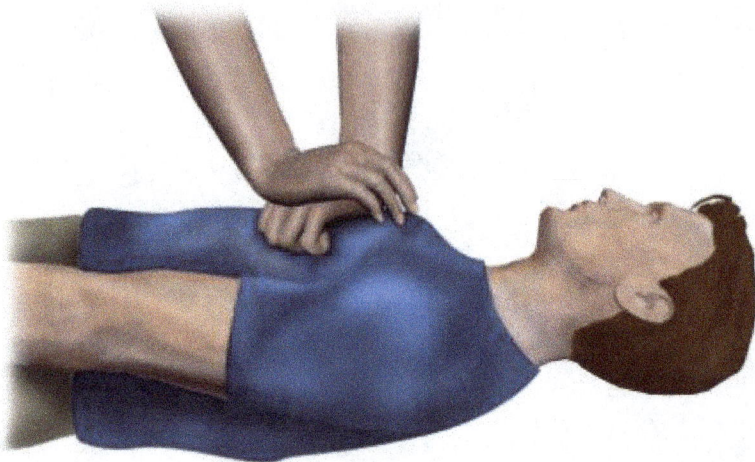

Position Hands Over Sternum

You should then take your other hand (one not holding the person's hand) and slowly move it towards the body and under the chin. Use both hands to grasp the collar and slowly pull the skin down and away from the mouth area. You should also remember to hold your breath and to relax your whole body. It's best to use one hand, preferably the left, to help support the other. Hold the person's pulse points with your fingers and then use the thumb and the index finger of your other hand to gently guide the first aid needle through the blood.

When you know how to perform DIY first aid, you'll be able to use the knowledge to help keep yourself or your friend alive until the paramedics can arrive.

First Aid in wilderness

Have you ever been out in the woods and slipped with your knife or cut yourself with your hatchet and you thought "oh crumb, I forgot my first-aid kit, what am I gonna do now?" So, you're still lost in the wilderness and a bear ate your first aid kit. What do you do? First thing, if you're injured presumably that bear that stole your kit also roughed you up a bit.

You need to clean the wound. Water will do fine for that, but preferably purified water should be your go-to. Obviously we have the ability with a water bottle to cleanse a wound. Next, you'll need some kind of bandage, use a piece of clean cloth or material to cover the wound and apply pressure cooling it down.

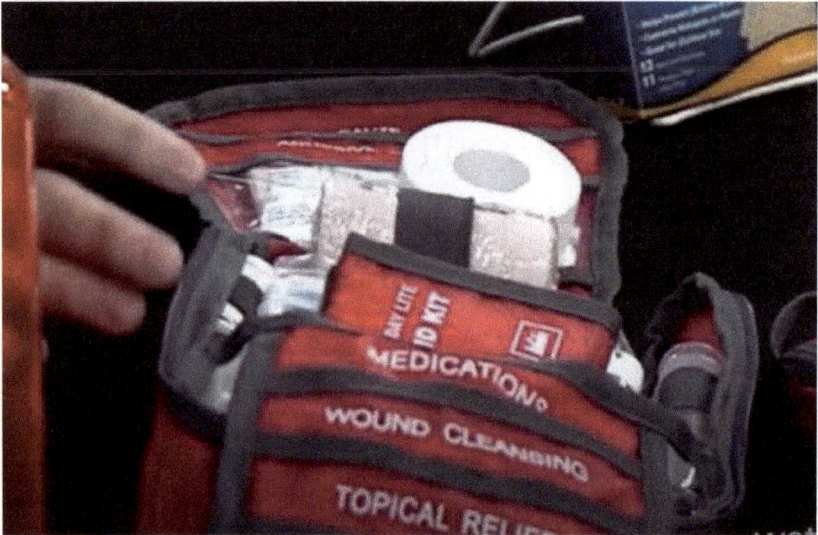

You can cool it down with mud, you can cool it down with sphagnum moss which grows all around in the wild. So, you can pack it with moss, you can wrap it with a t-shirt that gives you compression. If you have duct tape to hold the bandage on, that's even better.

Now you'll need to find some old man's beard don't worry, it's a type of lichen, it's green and it grows on tree branches.

You can apply that to your wound as an antibiotic and you should be good to go depending on how serious the wound is.

For those who need more instruction, contact your local emergency medical service. Do yourself a favor and learn how to perform first aid before you try to save somebody else's life.

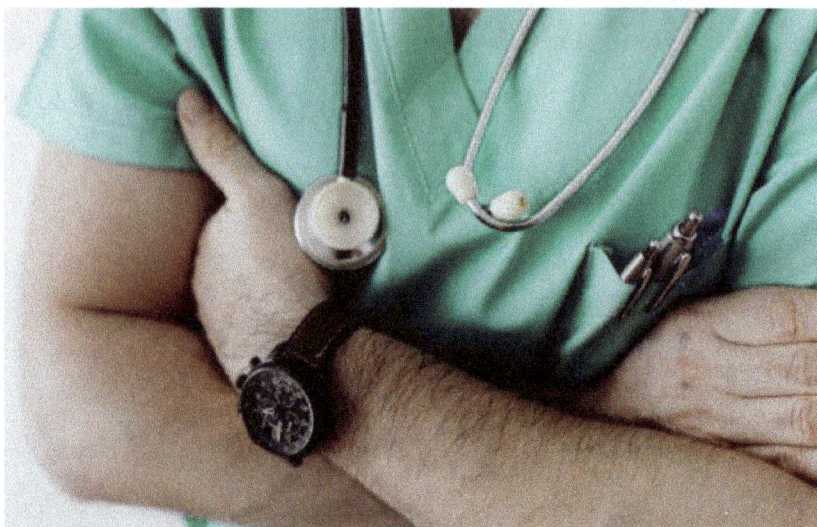

You could learn to do it in a hurry if you weren't afraid of heights!

Number 6: How to Get Water From Plants in Jungle Environments

If you've ever been to the Amazon, South America or other places where people live by the water, you'll know how important it is to get water from plants.

Getting water from plants in jungle environments is not an easy thing to do. There are a lot of snakes, frogs and insects around. It can be dangerous even for the strongest of jungle warriors, if they don't have the right equipment.

In these types of situations, getting water from plants becomes very important. You will need to use a filtration system or something similar. And you'll also need to take special precautions just to stay safe.

So, let's say that you are in the Amazon, or in another environment like Central Africa. At first you may have to walk a long way to get water, depending on where you're going to try and get water from. The longer you walk, the harder it gets. Plus you may need to carry your equipment and water. Then you'll need to take into account the type of water you're trying to get. Do you need rain water? Do you need a pond water feature? Are you in an area where it rains a lot? Make sure that you have a way to purify the water, so that it will be safe for drinking.

Also when it comes to plants in jungle environments, you will need to think about getting a source of water. Many people will bring buckets, but remember that these are living creatures.

This means that insects and snakes could be getting into them and drinking their water. Also make sure you have a source for wastewater or sewage water.

These are just a few things to consider when it comes to how to get water from plants in jungle environments. If you live in an urban area where there is a large water supply, then you may not have to worry about these problems at all. However, if you live in a remote area that does not have many water sources available to you, then you will have to do what you can to keep them clean.

Number 7: Using Woodcraft to Make Chairs and Table etc.

Using woodcrafts to make Chairs and tables in a forest can be a very rewarding experience for children, teens and adults. If you have ever gone to a theme park then you know that most of the trees that are used to create these tables and chairs are live. Why? Because it is cheaper to use live objects than creating something from scratch and it is easier to do the woodcraft at the park.

Most theme parks use woodcrafts in a jungle themed setting. Most of us are familiar with the jungle animals and jungle themed decorating. This is also a perfect time to learn about the beauty of nature and how we need to care for it. Most of the furniture that you will see in a jungle themed area will be made of wood.

Woodcrafts such as chairs, tables and benches are very common. These items can easily be made using simple hand tools using simple woodcraft patterns. You can also learn how to use the various tools available to create a variety of fun jungle decorations. From picture frames, bird houses to furniture, there are lots of different things you can do with wood crafting in Wilderness.

The best way to learn how to make something is by doing it. Bring your own tools with you, or borrow them from a friend. Get some free advice from local people to - people who have been woodcrafting for many years. They will be able to help you make your first project.

The best material to use for this style of crafting is a soft wood such as pine or birch. You can even use cedar and Aspen. But you don't have to stick to pine or birch. As long as it's strong enough, you can use almost any wood you want.

The more detailed the plans, the easier woodcrafting in Wilderness will be. That means you should get some practice. Try making different styles of furniture. Or make a couple of different picture frames. Once you've mastered one design, move onto the next.

A good design always starts with a sketch. Draw the whole thing on graph paper first. Then bring that sketch to life on the piece of wood you're about to make. It's important to make sure your woodcrafting in Wilderness is as detailed as possible. It needs to be a true reflection of what you've imagined. Otherwise, you'll end up making a shoddy job of the wrong design.

When you're about to make something, think of the ways you can improve upon it. Use lighter or darker wood for different parts of a piece. Don't forget to make a rough sketch of your finished product. Then you can go back over it and change anything you think needs to be changed. You can also use woodcrafting in Wilderness to make crafts that other people will enjoy. Go online to find a group of people who enjoy woodcrafting. You can trade tips, ideas, designs and anything else you think can improve someone else's work. You can even make a few extra bucks by selling your pieces. It's possible to make some really good money with wood crafting in Wilderness. You don't need to be super-smarty or knowledgeable. You just need to have a little bit of patience and creativity. You can easily learn how to make crafts by taking classes or buying books on woodcrafting in Wilderness. Soon you'll be creating great products that others will admire.

It is important to remember that you should always learn about safety precautions when working with woodcrafts as these could prove to be very dangerous.

Number 8: Foraging Crayfish

One of the things that makes for a great day in the wilderness is fishing for Crayfish.

Unfortunately, if you are new to Crayfish Foraging then it can be quite a challenge, so before you start out foraging it would be a good idea to get to know your surroundings, know your fish and learn how to forage effectively, which is where a few tips come in.

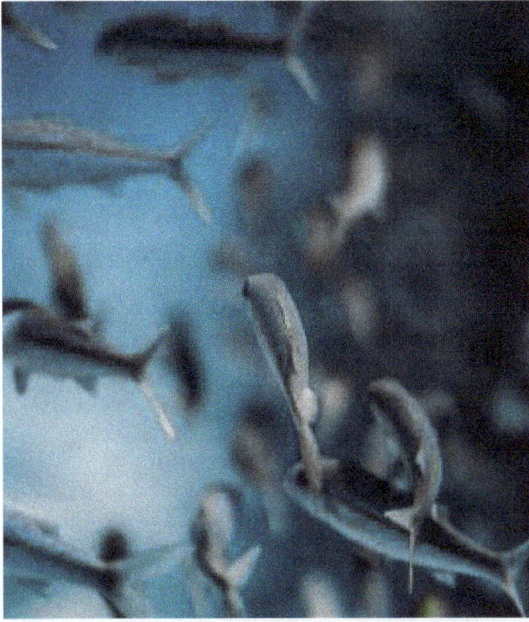

The biggest tip that you can use when foraging Crayfish in the wild is to know where they are likely to be located.

When foraging crayfish for the first time, it is important to keep a close eye on weather conditions. Foraging in this way during the summer months when it is hot, can be very rewarding, because you might catch quite a bit. However, if it is extremely cold, and raining you could be wasting valuable time.

Foraging Crayfish in the winter is also a great way to catch crayfish because you will have an easier time seeing them. If the foraging activity has stopped all together and you still have some opportunity to fish you should do so, but it is not essential to forage every minute and every second. For those who are new to Crayfish Foraging and are unfamiliar with their environment can sometimes find it difficult to determine where crayfish have been hiding.

If you have no man-made materials you can make traps from natural materials such as honeysuckle. Here is an example of one of these traps made by my friend from bush tools.

What if you have no man-made equipment or tools and you need to catch food fast, for this you can actually use nothing but your bare hands.

Crayfish like to live under rocks and boulders. If the clarity of the water is good, you can often spot them crawling around on the riverbed.

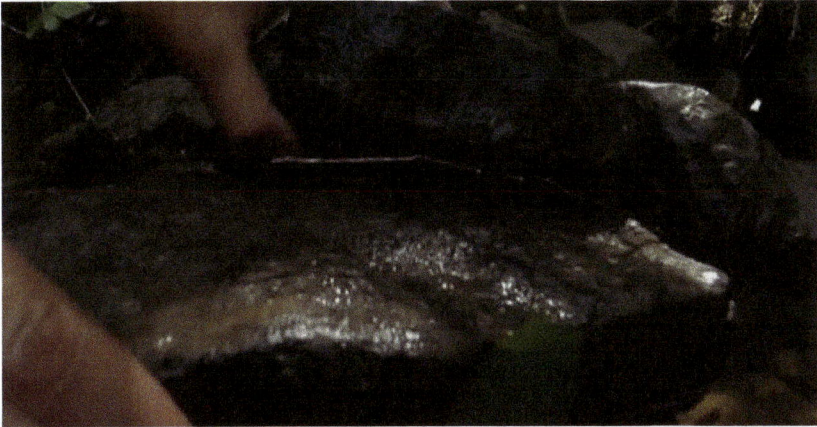

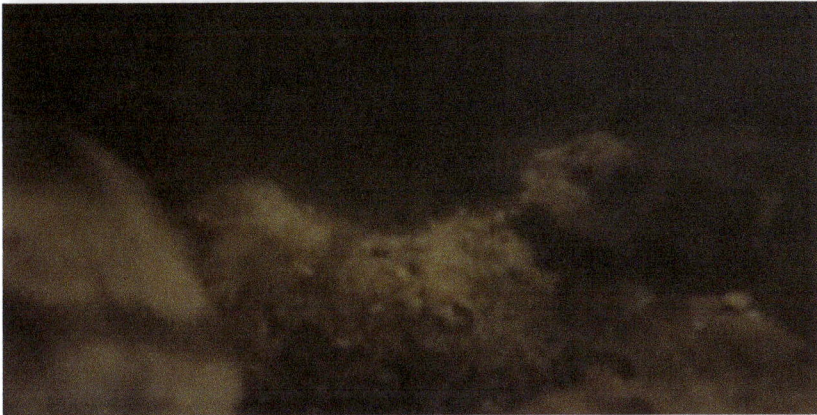

If you are quick you can pin them to the ground avoiding their pincers. They taste incredible and you can either boil them or cook them directly over a fire.

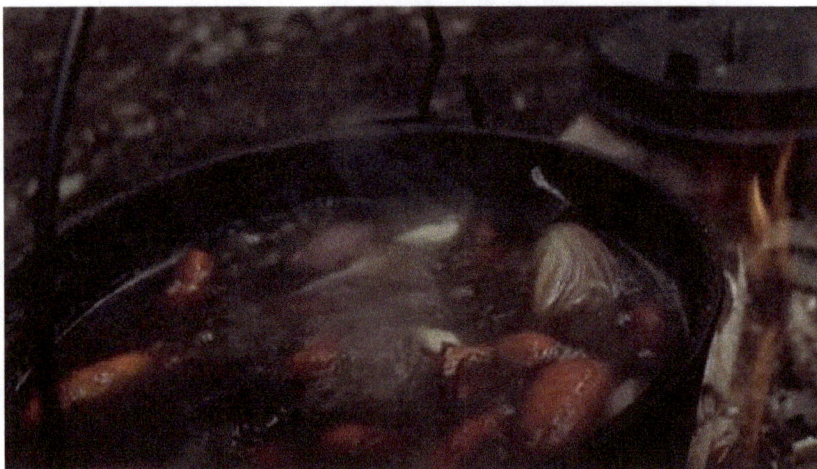

You should also try to use as many types of bait as possible while foraging for crayfish. Crayfish will generally eat any type of food, so try utilizing either live or frozen foods that they are accustomed to. If you are new to Foraging Crayfish, or even if you have been foraging crayfish for quite a long time, it may be a good idea to use jigs as well. Try using them as lures during some of your foraging trips.

Number 9: How to Build a Fire in Wildfire

One of the most fun activities is learning how to build a fire in the wilderness. Even if you are not fond of fire, you can build a fire easily as long as you follow some important tips. Here are some tips on how to build a fire in the wilderness. This will also help you make your own fire as well. Just follow these simple steps and you will be off to a great start.

Place stone around the place you have planned to build a fire. If there are some marshy lands nearby, then dig some holes in those for the stone to rest in. Make sure you cover all the places with sand to avoid the smell of wet wood. Step inside the holes and put the stone inside.

Step One: Using a small flat piece of wood, place a log inside the small hole and cover it with dirt. The dirt should be loose so that the log does not shrink or stick inside the small hole. Draw some lines around the log to show where the hole should be. Use a pencil to draw the lines clearly.

Step Two: Using larger sticks, place these around the log. Make sure you secure the sticks firmly with dirt. Once the soil is secure, use the flat piece of wood to support the logs. Windbreak the large sticks in around the log.

Step Three: Spread some tinder on the ground near the fire. When tinder becomes wet, it can start to ignite. If tinder still does not catch fire, cover the hole with dry twigs or dry branches. Use some clean dry cloth to wipe the surface of the rocks and the ground. Place your now ready-made firewood in the hole and light the tinder.

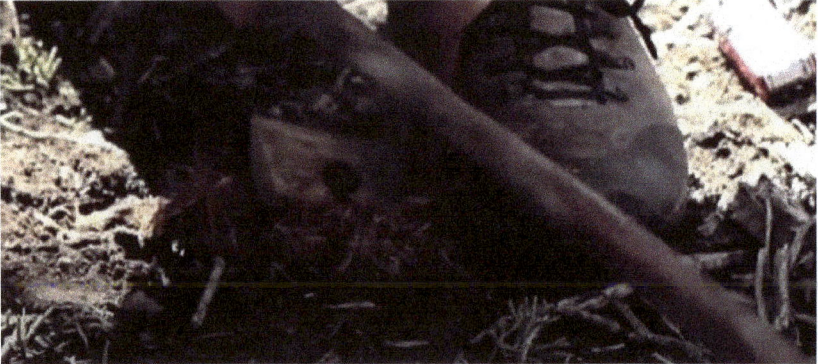

Step Four: Use some larger sticks to place around the fire as well as dry pine needles. Place them tightly against the rocks. Allow them to remain there for about thirty minutes. Once they are all burned, produce enough heat to start a small piece of coal. Light the coal and use this to start the process over again with the other pieces of wood.

Step Five: Build a fire in the wilderness that uses dry materials. Place some clean dry logs in the bottom of the fireplace and then build up more logs at the top. You will need enough wood for everyone involved. After you have built enough pieces for everyone, sprinkle some charcoal over them. Allow the charcoal to smolder for about twenty minutes before placing the fire back into the fireplace. When you do this process, you will begin to produce sparks from the fire.

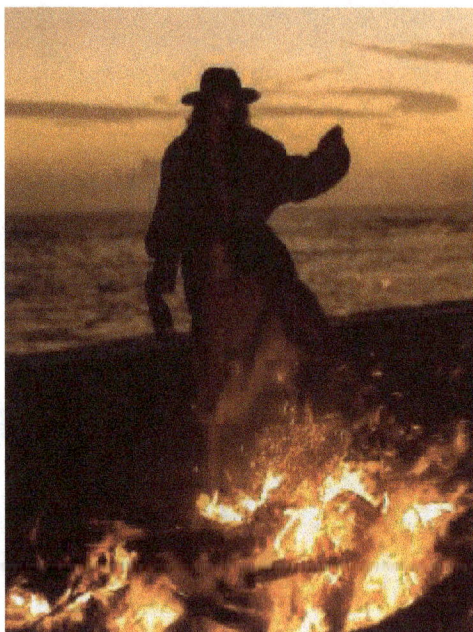

Step Six: If the wood has not produced any sparks, you may want to try using an electric bow to create them. If you are not comfortable firing the bow, then you can simply use a small piece of wood as well as some dried twigs or pieces of paper to create the fire. Place the wood at the top and then bring it down slowly over the open piece of paper. You can use the bow to help generate more and stronger sparks. Continue in this manner until you produce plenty of free hot coals.

Number 10: How to Gather moss in Forest - Use Nature's Resources

The best time of the year for collecting moss is in summer or fall when trees are producing their fruit and new growth is occurring.

The type of tree you get will affect how to gather moss in the forest, but there are several common types. Each has its own way of production that must be taken into consideration.

One of the most common types of moss is deciduous trees such as oak, birch and maple. This type of mosses is usually small and dark green in color and can grow on a tree without being noticed. It forms bundles or mats under the tree where it matures and releases itself in the air.

The easiest way to learn how to gather moss in the forest is to follow nature. Observe what trees in the area are producing and how many branches they have. The thicker the tree the more moss will grow and there are two types. One is needlelike and the other is scalloped.

Needlelike mosses grow in clusters and look like large mushrooms. They are usually very fine and powdery and can hide in the smallest spaces. Scalloped mosses are the thickest and can be spotted easily. The branches of this type of moss can reach very high and trees can collapse if the branches are weak or break off. There are many ways to determine whether a tree is needlelike or scalloped and you can do so by taking a branch and examining it closely.

If you are learning how to gather moss in forest one important aspect is moisture. You need to look for moisture either on the moss itself or in the soil beneath it. Moisture will help the moss grow and spread out but if it is not kept up the moss will not spread. Moss in wet areas will start to shrink and if it is too much it will even die.

Collect as much moss as you can, it is worth preserving. If you find a good spot to collect then use it repeatedly to create new molds that will improve the quality of your moss. You can save the tree bark and the moss together and make a really unusual decorative mixture that will last a long time.

If you are looking to put the moss into a pot, then be sure that you will be able to dry it out before you place it into the pot. The first few times you try to mold moss, you may find that it keeps growing until you pour water on it, then you realize that the tree bark has died and the moss is ready to be used.

Chapter 2: Top 11 Survival Tips

Number 11: How to make a spear to catch animals and food

You've got a fish on your spear and are trying to stab it out to get him, to kill him so that you can bring him back but it ends up getting away. Here's a handy tip for catching cute little forest creatures or small marine animals for consumption.

A split tip gig is a multi pronged spear that quickly snatches critters from the forest floor or in a body of water. You want me to make a spear? We need you to make wonderful fishing. Find yourself a small sapling about an inch around and cut the thicker end into four parts.

Going about ten inches down from the top out, spread those tips up. Use a stick to spread the parts and then make sure they're good and sharp with a rock or knife. Finally, use that gigtube, we can spear anything from snakes to chipmunks - rats, raccoons, bears, fish etc.

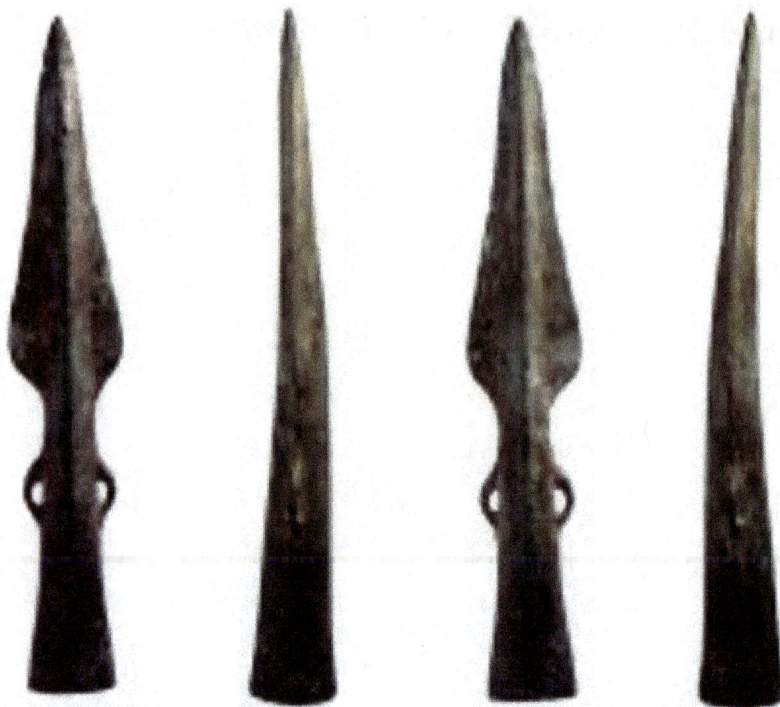

Learning how to make a spear to catch fish and animals in the wild is not as difficult as one may think. In fact, it can be quite easy, provided that you know how to handle your weapon properly. Spearheads can be in many different shapes and sizes, which make them great for hunters who want to use something more than just a stick or a branch to dispatch their prey. A spear is generally made out of metal or wood, but there are some materials out there now that are particularly effective in boating.

The first part is choosing the right type of spear. The most common type is a long stick, but there are also smaller ones available, as well as those that look more like the end of a hook. A spearfishing stick is typically made out of wood or metal and is either fixed in place or lightweight enough to be carried around. This is usually the best choice for those who are just starting out, as it is easy to learn how to use it. If you have experience, however, a fixed spearfishing pole is probably better since you will be able to get some practice using that while practicing your new skills.

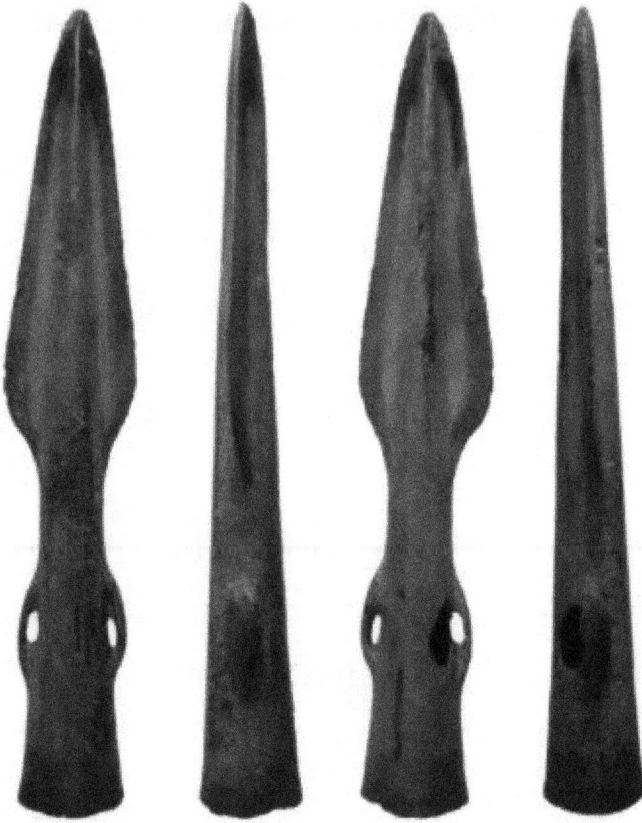

Once you have the right type of spear, you need to find where the fish are biting. This is an important part of learning how to make a spear to catch fish and is often done with the aid of a guide. A guide can help you find the best places to spearfish, so that you can stay safe and get the fish you want. If you are spearfishing in wild waters, you can sometimes even get away with not bringing your spearfishing equipment with you. This is because some rivers and streams do not have any restrictions on the type of equipment you can use, so long as it is not considered illegal or dangerous to use them. However, if you are spearfishing in a state park or another body of water that is off limits, make sure you bring your spear with you so you can be assured that it will remain legal.

It is also important that you take care of your spear. You do not want it damaged or scratched because it might come into contact with a sharp object, such as a bolt, hook, or other part of the fish's body. Before each use, wash the spear in hot soapy water. You can also wipe it down with a damp cloth to remove any soap residue or dirt that might accumulate on it. Wipe it down carefully, but try not to move it around too much, so that it does not become jagged or damaged.

If you learn how to make a spear to catch fish and practice using the proper techniques, you will find that you will be able to use this skill for many seasons to come. You might be surprised at how quickly you learn how to shoot your spear accurately and with little effort. You might even be able to go out in the wilderness and find fish right away, which is a very exciting feeling! Your friends might surprise you as well, because many people have heard of someone using a spear to catch fish, but never realized that they actually did it themselves.

Spear-fishing is fun, easy, and exciting. You should take the time to learn all of the basics that you can before heading out on your first trip. The wild world out there is waiting to feed on your success. Spearfishing is not a new sport, but it is one that has been growing in popularity lately. Now is the time that you discovered it, so that you can make the most of your time out on the water.

Number 12: How to find food?

When these are compact and green, you can eat those, some people who boil those up and cook them that way. If you don't have a split tip gig, you'll need to get food another way.

Before you become food for something else, your best bet is to find a guide that tells you which berries and flowers are edible. If one isn't handy which it probably isn't, if you're lost in the wilderness then you can use the good old fashioned method of trial and error.

Remember this rhyme 'white and yellow kill a fellow, purple and blue good for you'. But beware, while this approach might allow you to survive longer, it might also kill you immediately. Come on now! it's got to be a little cautious. I mean that book of yours is cool and everything but you can't depend entirely on leaves and berries.

If you'd rather not leave your survival to chance there are a few rules of thumb to adhere to avoid plants with milky or discolored SAP. 3 leaved growth patterns, almond scented leaves, anything like seeds that are inside pods and things that look like mushrooms.

Wild food sources are very important for our health and survival. There are many types of wild foods such as berries, nuts, wild greens, mushrooms, and many more. It is up to us to know how to find food in the wild for daily consumption.

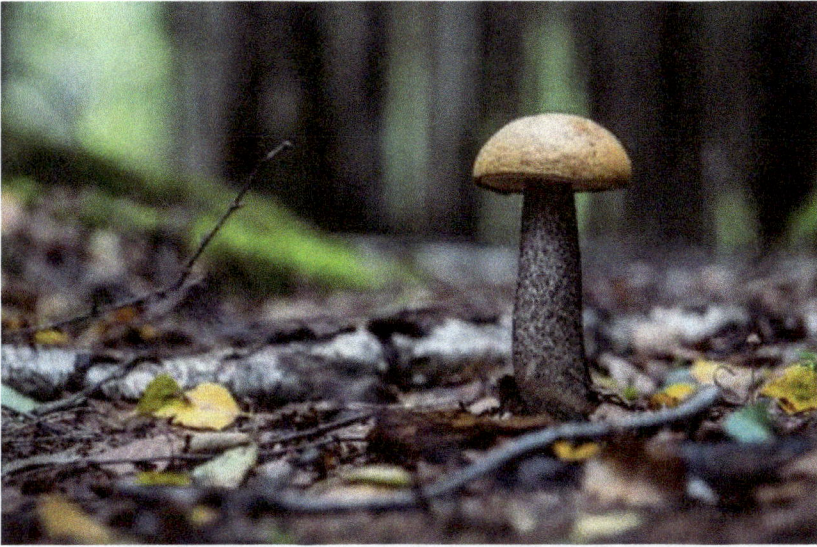

Many people want to have a wonderful vacation and experience nature. But many also want to do something for the environment so that we can all leave our trash in a better place instead of taking it on the trip and leaving it for dead or dying animals to eat.

If you are on a vacation in the wild and need some food for you to stay, you may wonder where you will find it. The answer is not difficult if you use your imagination. There are many sources of food in the wild that you can find while enjoying your vacation. One of these sources are insects.

There are many types of bugs and other insects that can be your food source while you are out there. They are usually easy to find because they are small and easy to miss. You may also be able to find other bugs that you can eat as well. Another food source is plant matter. There are many types of plants and some are edible. You may be able to find fruits and vegetables as your main food source as well.

When looking for a food source in the wild, you need to look around and see what you can forage for. Look for areas where there are insects feeding on the insects that live in your area. If you cannot find a food source in the wild there is another option of finding things that are edible.

You can find a variety of different foods from mushrooms to salami to squirrel repellents. If you can find these types of things you can eat them to get them back into shape for some of the times when you are not camping with your friends or family.

Camping can be a fun time for many people. However, you need to know how to find food in the wild west. It is important to take your food supply with you to camp, so you will have it once you get back from the campground.

The best way to find something edible to eat while you are in the wild west is to keep a food diary. Once you get familiar with the foods you will see the type of things that you will eat. Good luck!

Number 13: How to build a fire?

If you do manage to get some food, you might need a fire to cook it but even without food you need to keep yourself warm. First and foremost, you'll need tinder not the app although, we suppose that's one way to keep yourself warm.

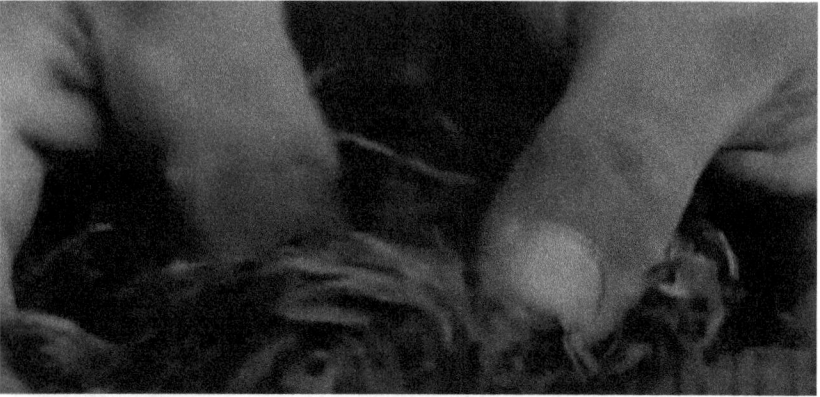

Tinder in this case refers to small stocks that will easily turn a spark into a full-blown fire. The best tinder you could use is a shareable tree bark.

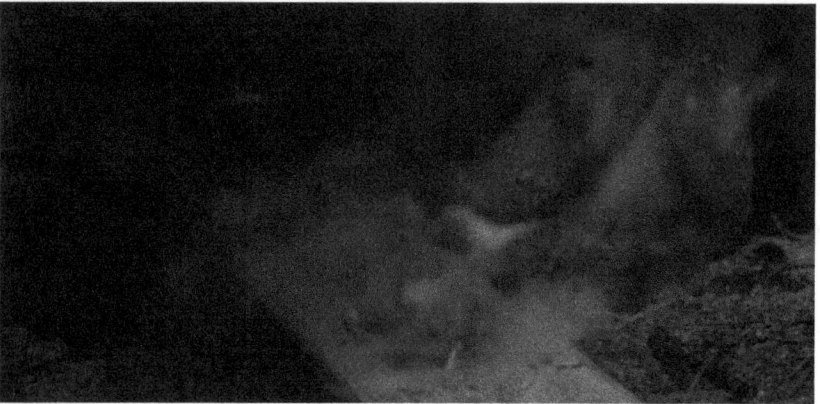

Break those up into even smaller bits, find an area to make your fire and create shelter from the wind by using a log or something big.

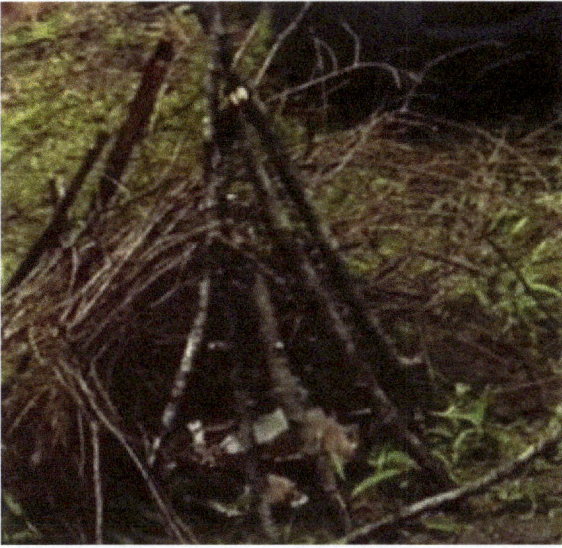

Then stack your kindling preferably branches of different sizes in a conical shape. This will facilitate the passage of oxygen to your fire which will make it grow. If you don't have any of the items mentioned in our signal fire entry, then you can use flint to spark the fire or again rub two sticks together.

When it starts to grow then you can begin to add bigger kindling. You could build fire extenders that would be things out of pine pitch or even birch bark or other easily ignitable material. Also don't forget to scavenge the area for any other material.

You can use it to keep yourself warm like leaves, pine branches or the skin of an animal you've hunted for food.

Number 14: How to build a shelter?

Well, It looks like you're gonna be here for a while and may as well get comfortable. You'll need to find a dry area preferably one that's flat elevated and protected from the elements. By a cliff wall look around for a strong tree.

Seeing white oak trees and pale models to build with this is a good spot. Ideally you want your tree to be at an angle but if that's not the case then grab a big branch from the ground, lean it against a strong tree and start stacking smaller branches on one side to make a wall.

Once, this is done, find leaves moss and other forest debris and start covering the wall as well as the ground to keep you warm. When you're finished, get cozy and pray that the wind doesn't pick up. This is what I might call a backwoods timeshare. No honorable mentions this time.

Wild animals have been our friends for a long time and it is our responsibility to look after them in the wild. They will come to harm in our homes but what else can we do.

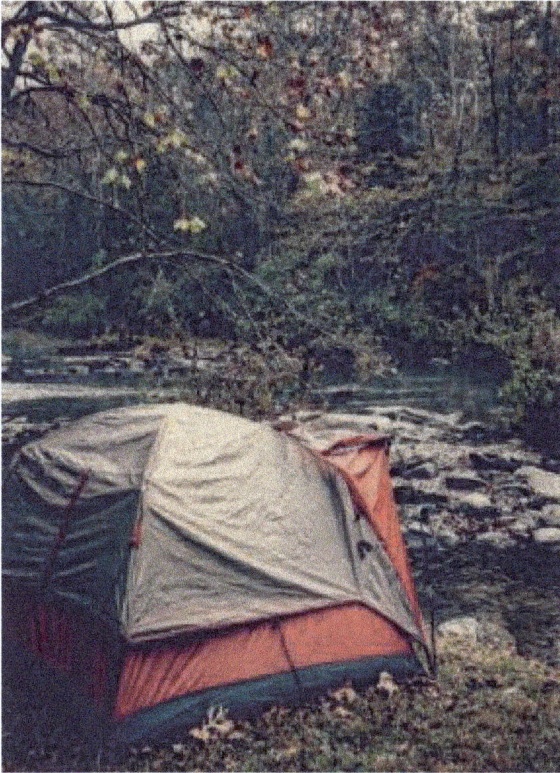

When I was a kid I used to watch my dad putting up a shelter for the birds. There is nothing more beautiful than watching birds and squirrels in their natural habitat. It is easy to build a shelter on your own but you need to be sure that you have all the building materials that you need.

The shelter does not always need to be outdoors, you can build one in your backyard. If you live in an area that has cold winters then you need to build a shelter that will protect you from the cold winter weather. There are so many different kinds of shelters that you can build and I would suggest that you visit your local stores and see what they have to offer you.

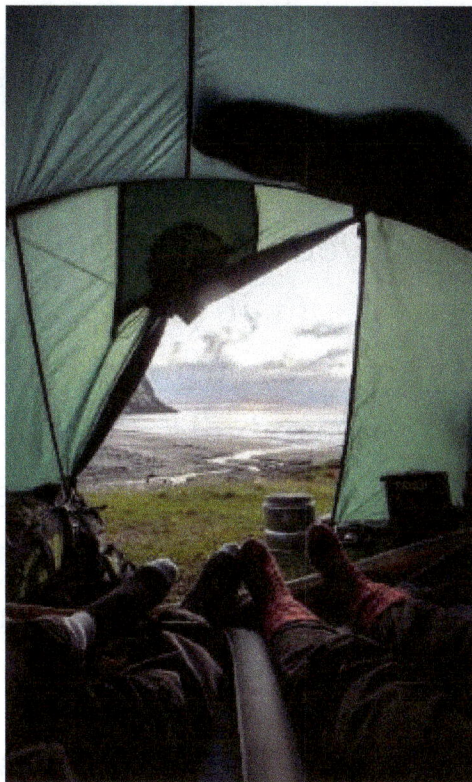

The shelter that you build will depend on the size. A big shelter will probably take a lot of work to build. You will need to build it at least ten feet higher than the ground so that animals cannot get into the shelter. Smaller shelters need to be built in such a way that they are level. If you build a shelter with uneven ground then animals could easily slip through the cracks. You should also make sure that you secure the foundation of the shelter to prevent water from flooding inside it.

You can build a shelter anywhere in your yard as long as you have enough room. You do not need to put it on top of anything because the ground is usually enough for it to stand on. You can build a wooden shelter or you can use stone. Both of these shelters will give shelter from the wild animals and you do not even have to worry about termites.

If you are a handyman or woman, then I would highly recommend building your own shelter. It is not as hard as you think it is. All you need is the right plans and a little bit of building experience. You can learn how to build a shelter in wild animals by searching the internet or checking out some books at your local library. There are a lot of great places to find information on how to build a shelter in less than an hour. You can be up and building a shelter in no time at all.

Building your own shelter is a great project for the kids to do. It gives them responsibility and teaches them how to be responsible. They can learn a lot by taking care of the wild animals that live in your yard. It will also teach them about nature. If you are someone who likes to spend time outdoors, then building a shelter is a great project for you to take on. I am sure that once you learn how easy it is to build a shelter for your animals, you will never want to go back to the store bought versions again.

Number 15: How to Find Clean Water

If you want to find water you must first find dirt. There's probably nothing more important to your survival than good fresh water.

That you find in a puddle or stream is a safe bet but only if you boil it. We told you that fire would come in handy, if you can't do that then collecting rain snow or Dew is also a great way to get yourself something drinkable.

To get enough of the stuff to keep you alive, you can soak the liquid using a rag or some type of fabrics like a shirt or bandana. Then squeeze the water out. You can also tie a bag around a leafy branch to collect the water from a tree's transpiration which is also drinkable. If you happen to find a cactus, you can slice it open for some refreshing h2o as well. Because there's so much of this that's where getting the fluid through, just a munch and suck finally and perhaps most deliciously. You can also quench your thirst with the syrup from a maple tree, awesome! What it boils down to is that staying safely hydrated is the name of the game with any luck at all in a few hours so long as the sun stays out.

Number 16: How to Light Fire With Flint and Steel

I remember when I was a child, my father always told me that if I wanted to do something dangerous, I should not try to do it on my own. He used to say that there would be too much danger involved in fire. So, I never did anything crazy or experimental until I was older. But, when it comes to learning how to start a campfire and start lighting the fire, many people wonder the same thing.

You can make use of either flint or steel for the fire starting materials. You should call for any help that is available if you don't know anything and make sure that you are safe.

You may be wondering how to start a fire with flint and steel? You should know that it is actually not that difficult if you follow some basic steps. If you follow these steps carefully, then you will surely have a good time during camping trips, barbeques, and other recreational activities.

First of all, you should gather all the flints that you need. You can use paper or cardboard to keep them in one bundle. The bundle should include several pieces of flint such as split pieces of flint, flakes, sand, and small pieces of shavings. Make sure that you have enough pieces of flint so that you will not run out while you are trying to start a fire.

After you have gathered all the flints, you should also make use of some newspaper to soak up the water that is left over after you have started to heat up the fire. It is important that you cover up the newspaper so that the smoke and smoky residue will not fall into the food that you will serve. Once the fire has already started, you should cover your nose and mouth so that you will not breathe in the smoke. You can also use a face mask if you do not feel comfortable breathing in smoke.

After you have covered your nose and mouth with the paper, you should remember to inhale the steam from the steel pan through your teeth. You should take a few deep breaths in order to bring the steam to your mouth and throat. Inhaling the steam will help you relax your body muscles and it will also help to clear the sinuses. You must remember to keep your hands away from the flames. Once you have done these things, you will be able to get the job done right and you will never be confused about whether you should continue or stop.

Number 17: Retaining water in Wild

There are many techniques you can use to locate and collect water. Sometimes a simple understanding of geography might be all that you need to take this shot. For example, you will notice a valley with two steep sides, this v-shaped valley was formed hundreds of thousands of years ago by glaciers carving their way through the softer rock. What it leaves behind is these valleys in the shape of a 'V'. At the base of these valleys there is a very high chance that you will find a river stream or some form of flowing water. But how do you find water in areas where there are no fresh running rivers, streams or lakes? The climate you're in is hot and arid. If you have a plastic bag, you can tie this around some leaves at the tip of branches on small trees and shrubs.

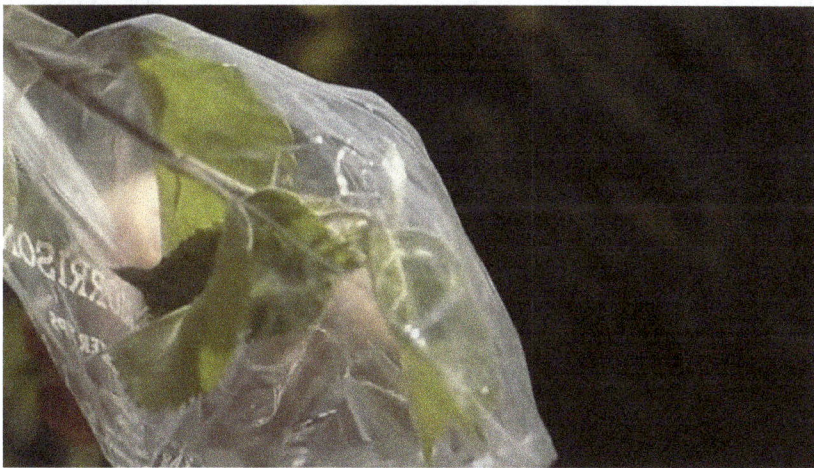

Wait a few hours and the sun will encourage evaporation to take. This water vapor that comes out of the leaves will begin to condense and water droplets will begin to form on the inside of the bag. In this example, it is the beginning of June and the outdoor temperature is 24 degrees Celsius you can see that within 10 minutes of placing this bag on the leaves. It's beginning to show condensation and just a few hours later you can begin to see water droplets forming on the inside of the bag although not much. These might well be the vital few drops of water you need to survive.

If you have no containers to collect water you can either use a tarp or even use any cloth type material. Hang it out in the rain and allow it to absorb water afterwards wringing it out to collect the rainwater it will hold this water for a while so you can carry it with you.

As you move you can also make a wooden cup from a small log just split it into four sections, carve a small notch in the bottom end of these sessions.

Number 18: Creating a Ferrocerium Rod Fire

There are many different ways to light a fire. Fire has helped humans to survive for thousands of years and it is still used to this day in our everyday lives.

The ability to be able to light a fire in the wilderness is one of the most essential skills that you can have in a survival situation. If you have a ferrocerium rod in your kit you can light so many different types of natural materials.

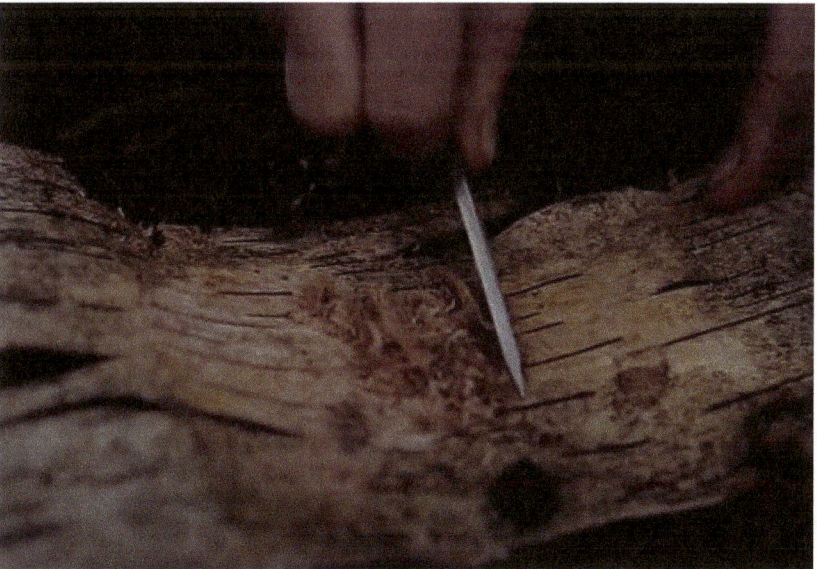

One of the best and most effective pieces of natural material for this is the bar from a silver birch tree.

Simply scrape the outer bark into small shavings. Shower it with sparks from your Ferro rod and it won't be long until you have a flame. This can also be done in wet conditions, when the bark is done.

Number 19: Light fire by Bow drill method

The next method is primitive fire by friction technique. A common friction fire lighting method is the bow drill. Using a thin stick as a spindle at another stick, cut to a flat shape to make a half board. You can begin to make your fire. You will need another stick to make your bow using some cordage.

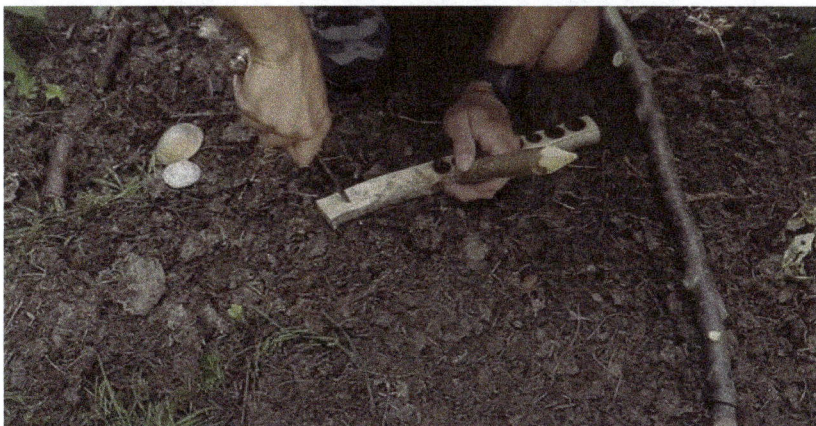

Wrap this around at both ends of your bow and attach it to your spindle. By twisting it, burning the board first with a few slow and consistent movements. Cut a small notch with your knife. This is for collecting the dust that you will create once your hearth board is ready. Begin to work the bow and spindle back and forth increasing downward pressure.

As you do so, when you start to see smoke don't stop, keep going for a few more seconds. You should have yourself an ember. Allow this Emberto establish and then place it in a tinder bundle and blow it to flame. Getting the ember is not the hard part but getting the ember turning into a flame can be tricky.

There are a few factors that you need to consider such as the type and dryness of the wood that you are using. Plus the climate and conditions that you are in practice in humid conditions, cold conditions and wet conditions.

But what if you have no cordage to make a total, how do you then light a fire? The hand drill is an even more rudimentary form of a bow drill and it is much harder to master.

It still utilizes the same principles through friction heat and oxygen to help you get that flame.

Number 20: Foraging Wild Edibles

It takes time and patience to learn this method, but it is a key survival skill to know having the knowledge of where your food comes from and how it arrives on your dinner plate.

Every day is something that we should all have a good understanding of. The ability to harvest your own food from the wild is key to turning a survival situation into a comfortable thriving environment.

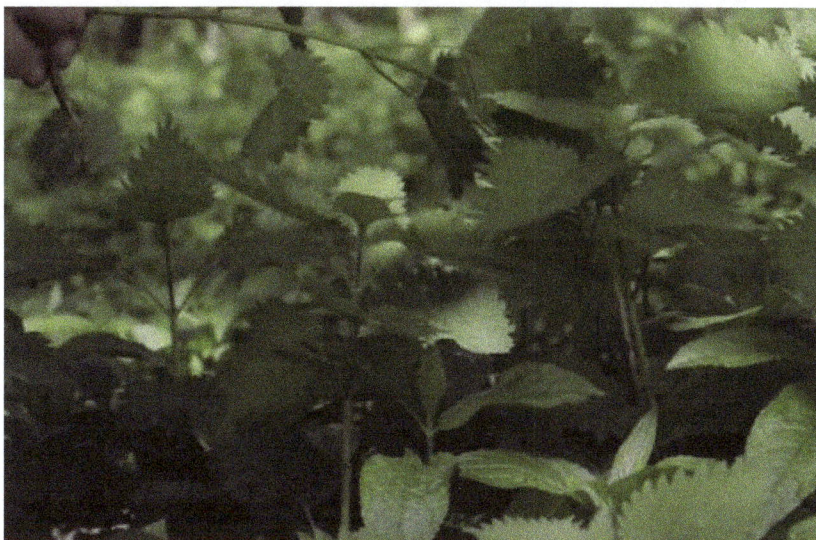

Having a good foundation knowledge of basic wild edibles is a good place to start, as you generally won't need any tools or equipment to gather them. For example, the humble stinging nettle Ithaca diosa. Despite its appearance and all-too-common stinging properties, it's actually packed full of vitamin A, Vitamin C, iron, potassium, manganese, and calcium.

In its peak season, nettle contains up to 25% protein dry weight which is high for a leafy green vegetable.

The leaves can also be dried and used to make herbal tea. It has been used to treat disorders of the kidney, cardiovascular system, influenza and gastrointestinal tract.

The stem of the plant contains bast fiber which can be used to make cordage. There are many more uses for this plant. However you cannot survive on nettles alone at some point. You will need to up the fat and protein content in your diet. So, that your body doesn't waste away.

Number 21: Drop Net Method

Another form of catching your own food is by net. The net can be incredibly effective when placed in the right area but this is more of a passive fishing technique.

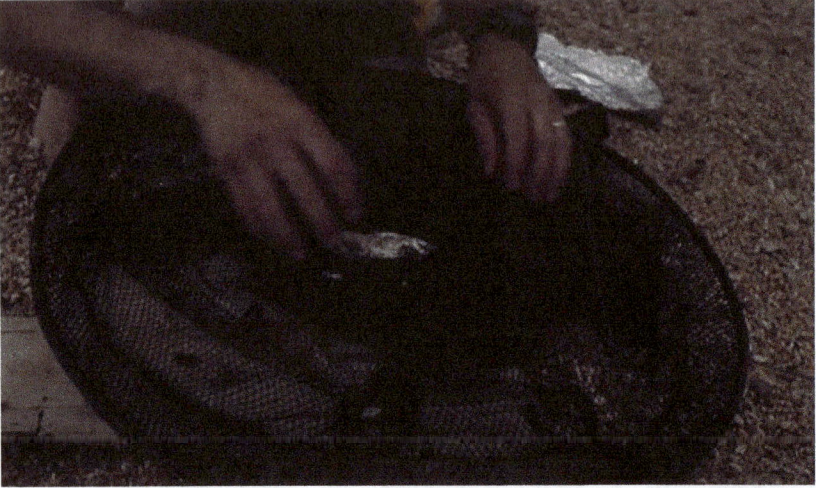

A drop net however can be a great way to catch crustaceans such as crab and lobster.

Simply put some bait in the net, making sure it is secure and drop it down to the sea bed. After 30 to 40 minutes, pull the net up to check your bait. If you want to be more active with your foraging, swim down and grab your crustacean directly from the net.

The benefit of this form of fishing and foraging is that you can drop multiple nets across a wide area giving you a greater chance of catching fish.

Conclusion:

When you combine all of these four pillars i.e fire, water, food and shelter together that's when you can begin to thrive which leads on to the fifth and final pillars of survival and that is the ability to thrive. Once you have access to food, fire, water and shelter you can begin to make life more comfortable for yourself. For example you can use bushcraft and woodcraft to create tables, chairs benches, cooking grains, pot hangers and much more. This will help you to keep your mind occupied and it will allow you to focus on thriving in the environment that you're in. Techniques to survive in the wilderness are easy if you know how to use them. Another technique to build your survival skills in the wilderness is to build shelter. Shelter can be as simple as a plastic tent to a cabin or log house. It should be well-built enough to withstand any weather condition. You can also learn to build your own emergency kit in the wilderness. This is essential especially if you encounter an emergency situation in the middle of wilderness. For example, if you come across a body of water, you should have a raft or a boat in order to safely cross it. In the same way, a bear should also be caged. This can be done by hanging a rope around his neck and a big stick over his eyes.

Thank you for reading this book. If you enjoyed it please share it with your friends.

CPSIA information can be obtained
at www.ICGtesting.com
Printed in the USA
BVHW051356080321
601998BV00011BA/1184